PREVENTING DERAILMENT: WHAT TO DO BEFORE IT'S TOO LATE

PREVENTING DERAILMENT: WHAT TO DO BEFORE IT'S TOO LATE

Michael M. Lombardo
Robert W. Eichinger

Center for Creative Leadership
Greensboro, North Carolina

The Center for Creative Leadership is an international, nonprofit educational institution founded in 1970 to foster leadership and effective management for the good of society overall. As a part of this mission, it publishes books and reports that aim to contribute to a general process of inquiry and understanding in which ideas related to leadership are raised, exchanged, and evaluated. The ideas presented in its publications are those of the author or authors.

The Center thanks you for supporting its work through the purchase of this volume. If you have comments, suggestions, or questions about any Center publication, please contact John R. Alexander, President, at the address given below.

Center for Creative Leadership
Post Office Box 26300
Greensboro, North Carolina 27438-6300

Center for
Creative Leadership

leadership. learning. life.

©1989 Center for Creative Leadership
Reprinted March 2002

Cover design by Bob Burke and Laura Gibson
Text design and layout by Joanne Ferguson

CCL No. 138
ISBN 0-912879-36-X

Table of Contents

How to Use *Preventing Derailment*

For managers and human resource professionals

1. To understand the dynamics of success and derailment, and how to prevent derailment through active development of managers.

2. To help determine who may be in danger of derailing and set up an intervention process.

3. To set up a system for management development which emphasizes comprehensive feedback, variety in leadership challenges and assistance in learning new management behaviors.

For individual development

1. To consider one's own derailment potential.

2. To provide recommendations for taking charge of one's own development through comprehensive feedback, variety in leadership challenges, and becoming a more active learner of new management behaviors.

Introduction

Many of the strengths that lead high-potential managers to early promotions become weaknesses. Many new managers, for example, rely too heavily on the technical or problem-solving strengths that have propelled them upward and fail to understand the interdependence required, or the diversity of what they must cope with in order to continue to be effective as managers.

The problem arises for both individual and organizational reasons and results in many managers failing to make the transitions required to deal with the increasing complexity they face. When this happens, many managers whose careers have been full of promise stumble. They derail.

Derailment is neither topping out nor opting out nor not winning a promotion each time one is available. It is reserved for that group of fast-track managers who want to go on, who are slated to go on, but who are knocked off the track. Such managers are demoted, plateaued early, or fired. Somewhere within the organization a group decides that they have failed to meet expectations and their careers go into eclipse (McCall & Lombardo, 1983; Lombardo & McCauley, 1988a).[†]

Much derailment is an organizational and a human waste that in our experience is largely preventable. This article is aimed at a specific population, those with potential for future leadership and executive roles who show early signs of not making it. Additionally, our recommendations focus on effective learning practices in management roles and have broader application for management development in general.

To apply a model of development to the special case of derailment, we will first discuss how development occurs or doesn't, then focus on who derails and why.

Second, because this article is intended for use, we will divide the remainder into two overlapping sections covering individual and organizational intervention.

In the first, Derailment: The Individual Face, we will introduce a high-potential manager, Michelle, at the point where she first runs into trouble, and invite readers to complete a derailment checklist on her. We will then discuss what was done to help her in the context of a model of management development and note other derailment patterns, as she represents only one type of potential derailer.

[†] Success was defined as being promotable, promotable with no place to go, or having achieved the level expected of the person. Those who "plateau" voluntarily, who take themselves out of contention, were not included in either group.

We will then turn to Derailment: The Organizational Face, to present eight recommendations for heading off the Michelles before they get into trouble and promoting more systematic development in organizations.

These two sections are intentionally somewhat repetitious. In the first we attempt to answer the question: "I've already got a potential derailer on my hands—what do I do Monday?" In the second, we attempt to answer the question: "How can organizations design practices to prevent derailment and help develop managers more fully?"

How Executives Develop

How is it that future executives develop on the job? Do certain experiences matter? Do they, as many have said, teach valuable lessons? Seeking answers to these questions has been the subject of continuing studies at the Center for Creative Leadership since 1982. To highlight four major conclusions of these studies (McCall, Lombardo, & Morrison, 1988):

- Executives believe that much is learned on the job, and similar lessons (skills, values, and life perspectives) were reported in every corporation studied. Learnings that executives say made a lasting impact on how they manage appear to be pervasive.

- The experiences that teach these lessons also have some predictability to them. Challenging job assignments, significant other people, hardships such as personal mistakes and failures or enduring hard times and setbacks, along with coursework at pivotal moments dominate what executives and managers recall as developmental.

- There is a strong link between experiences and lessons learned. What is learned is not random; it flows from the specific experience. For example, a common challenging job assignment is having to turn around a troubled unit. Regardless of corporation (or nationality in some instances), managers reported similar learning patterns.

- Having the experience is far from a guarantee of new learning. Only managers who continued to be effective added new patterns of management behavior; others who derailed often had the same experiences but missed the meaning. The derailed managers either relied too heavily on successful habits or exhibited flaws which acted as blocks to their learning. The essence of learning from experience, then, is in overcoming comfortable habits and personal quirks and making transitions to new ways of behaving.

For example, a common lesson for successful executives from tackling a too-big job is that development of others is a necessity. To learn to do something differently they focused on helping subordinates problem find so they could figure out what to do for themselves. In contrast, executives who later derailed relied on past habits—they focused upward, looking to the boss for help, then sought to control downward by instituting more systems and working longer hours.

Both groups had the same leadership challenge, both were elite groups, and the learning overlap concerning the development of others was 0%. The danger for any of us is that we will meet a new situation with old behavior, behavior that has served us well so far. Even for men and women who reach the top 1% of positions in their organizations, learning new patterns of behavior is far from automatic.

Overall, the CCL studies concluded that confronting variety in leadership challenges and overcoming our successful habits, quirks, and flaws to make transitions to new ways of behaving and thinking is what separated the successful and the derailed in a group of 400 executives. Those who benefited from experience could develop into more balanced people, able to be tough and compassionate, able to lead and let others lead when necessary. This flexibility was again only made possible by experience; it was hardly guaranteed, even for successful executives.

In the world executives describe, there are few constants. Skills and qualities are mutable—strengths become weaknesses, skills change, and the job context in which they play out is critical. Any future CEO comes into an organization with some basic platform skills—basic intelligence, good schooling, and probably some solid interpersonal skills. Then the forging process begins; regardless of the skills a person brings to the party it is the playing out of these skills and values and perspectives in tough situations that make the difference. During a career any future CEO will probably deal with hateful bosses, learn marketing in an unknown business while dealing with a balky staff and a decaying market share, shut down operations, fire long-term loyal employees, learn to understand hard-to-understand people so problems can be solved without bloodshed, commit numerous blunders and deal with shovel-in-the-face crises.

To speak of successful executives is to speak of those who learned their trade in the fires of experience. Their overwhelming response when explaining why an experience was developmental was that the stakes were high, the last person who tried it failed, their boss wasn't helpful and so on. They grew and changed primarily when they had to.

Knowing what to do or demonstrating our skills or our humanity in low-stakes situations tells us little and teaches us little because our past habits basically still work. Significant learning seems to require significant pressure. New management learning would certainly be a snap for future executives if it weren't for the stress and uncertainty which are also the same conditions that make new learning so precious because it's so difficult to give up old habits and to overcome our numerous quirks.

Although any of us are loathe to give up the successful habits of the past, those who derail are particularly likely to cling to behavior that is becoming less effective. In the next section we'll examine what these people look like and how they get to be that way.

Those Who Derail

Perhaps 30-50% of high-potential managers and executives derail,[†] and this group is often not identical to the general management population. Those who wish to lead, as Doug Bray and Ann Howard found, like to "take charge of things in group situations and propel the group toward its goals. They tend to be dissatisfied with a subordinate role. They are more independent and less affiliative" (Bray & Howard, 1988). Similarly, Bernard Bass in his work on high-performing leaders found them to be assertive, introspective, have high energy and initiative, and the ability to solve problems well and quickly (Bass, 1985).

Such people are common in the fast tracks in organizations with their obvious strengths of taking charge and solving problems well. With these strengths, they often carry corollary weaknesses: They are often impatient, don't listen well, are independent to the point that work relationships suffer, and like to solve problems alone. Such personality characteristics work well at lower levels where jobs are more technical and individual problem solving is rewarded, but later in a career technical proficiency matters less than the

---

[†] Sorcher (1985) estimates failure rates as high as 33% for senior executives; two companies in the CCL studies had rates of 50% involuntary turnover across a five-year period for high-potential managers and executives.

ability to deal with a variety of leadership situations, only some of them technical in nature, and independence is less valued than interdependence and teamwork.

In a sense they and the organizations that grow them are continuing the leadership development of the past, where technical skills and control were highly valued. Organizations in the 1950s, for example, were more independent of outside competition and had more homogeneous beliefs in the workforce. Only 20% of American businesses faced international competition versus over 70% in the 1980s (Peters, 1987). New competition and rapid technological change means new clients, new products, and immense complexity. Technical proficiency and control worked well for mature products, slow change, and broad markets, but has given way to the interdependence of diverse units and the need to deal with diverse situations and people in the modern organization. In a world where 85% of Digital Equipment Corporation's profits come from products introduced in the past 24 months, quick innovation and the need for teamwork dominate (Peters, 1987).

This increased competition and sheer rate of change has occurred along with changes in motivation in the workforce. With increasing affluence and concern for quality of life, Manny London of AT&T notes broad differences between the recruits of today and 20 years ago. "New managers have a greater desire to give and receive emotional support and are less certain that management is their best career choice. High need for achievement and low need for advancement seem to typify the new breed. These individuals desire challenging jobs which allow them to pursue their non-work interests" (London, 1983).

The complexity and fragmentation of the modern organization and its markets mirrors the changes in motivations and beliefs of its constituencies. In the Center for Creative Leadership's studies of learning from experience across a number of organizations, the three major effectiveness factors found reflect the changing demands placed on leaders. More effective leaders were (see Appendix for a complete listing):

- More adaptable to change, dealt better with ambiguity and complexity, and learned more quickly from a variety of experiences.

- Able to build teams in a variety of circumstances with many different types of people.

- Characterized by respect for self and others. They sought out feedback, delineated their strengths and weaknesses, likes and dislikes. Knowing themselves enabled them to both appreciate others and develop compassion for the inevitable limitations both they and others had. (McCauley, Lombardo, & Usher, forthcoming)

As the demands of leadership have changed, so has what leaders need to be to meet those demands. The balances have slid away from technical certainties to dealing with complex, ambiguous leadership situations; from independence to interdependence and team-building; and from directiveness to mutual understanding.

As the face of leadership has changed so has the face of derailment. On page 7 are the reasons found for derailment in CCL research (Lombardo & McCauley, 1988a), all of which reflect the flip side of one or more of the effectiveness factors above. Those who are not adaptable may get into trouble for failing to make transitions; those who are independent to a fault may be weak team-builders; those who develop a limited knowledge of self may become overdependent or treat others poorly.

As noted earlier, the most visible group of derailers are those high in independence and low in affiliation needs who tend to be seen as bright, technically proficient problem-solvers with poor team-building skills. But this is only the most visible of the types. The CCL studies suggest that many other types of derailers exist. Of the six major flaws cited, the typical derailer is cited for two of the flaws, making for many permutations and combinations in derailment. On pages 8-9 are first listed some typical early strengths which may get managers placed on the fast-track. Beside them are the latent weaknesses and untested areas these strengths often hide. The next column indicates some of the changing expectations placed on managers across time and the final column shows how those early strengths rewarded and untempered by further development may derail a manager. Because many possible combinations exist, these patterns are suggestive, not inclusive. All were cited as actual patterns, however, in CCL derailment research.

The Process of Derailment

With the exception of unforgivable sins—dishonesty or breaches of integrity—derailment patterns play out over time. Standards of excellence change as managers who were first rewarded for standout individual contributions are later expected to orchestrate a network, team build, and see that things are done rather than do many tasks alone.

Why Managers Derail

1. **Difficulty in molding a staff:**
   - slapdash selection, cronyism, or choosing staff in one's own image;
   - being dictatorial with subordinates;
   - not resolving conflict among subordinates;
   - being a poor delegator.

2. **Difficulty in making strategic transitions.** This becomes particularly apparent when entering the executive culture or switching to an unknown area (line to staff; new division or technical specialty) and involves:
   - folding under the pressure of a new culture or an ambiguous assignment;
   - not being able to deal with complexity—becoming mired in tactical issues or detail, or coming up with simplistic agendas;
   - failing to make the transition from doing to seeing that things are done.

3. **Lack of follow-through:**
   - lack of attention to essential detail, thereby creating a trail of little problems and disorganization;
   - speedboating along without really completing a job or leaving people dangling due to unmet promises;
   - often results in managers being described as untrustworthy.

4. **Poor treatment of others:**
   - overambition—bruising others on the way up or worrying more about getting promoted than doing the current job;
   - needing no one else—looking out for number one, being a know-it-all, making others feel stupid, and general isolation;
   - abrasiveness—bullying, general insensitivity, and lack of caring;
   - lack of composure—volatile and unpredictable under pressure.

5. **Overdependence:**
   - staying with the same boss or advocate until people wonder if the person can stand alone;
   - losing a shield when a person is separated from someone who compensated for a weak spot;
   - relying too much on a strength such as a skill, natural talent, or raw energy.

6. **Disagreements with higher management about how the business should be run or about strategy:**
   - inability to sell a position;
   - inability to adapt to a boss with a different style.

The Process of Derailment

EARLY STRENGTHS	LATENT PROBLEMS/ UNTESTED AREAS	CHANGING DEMANDS	MAY SLIDE INTO TROUBLE DUE TO...
1. Brilliant, driver, ambitious, high standards, tough on laggards.	a) overambitious, bruises others b) needs no one else c) abrasive d) lacks composure e) handles others' mistakes poorly f) doesn't know how to get the most out of people—appreciate what they can do	Interpersonal effectiveness, building and mending relationships, stability required for trust to develop	Poor treatment of others
2. Independent, likes to do it alone; *or* the opposite—overmanages, sits on subordinates extremely loyal to organization.	a) doesn't develop subordinates b) doesn't resolve conflict among subordinates c) poor delegator d) selects in own image e) has never chosen or built a staff	Team-building, staffing, developing others increase in importance	Can't mold a staff
3. Controlling, results-oriented, single-minded, really nails down technical detail; *or* extremely personable, relies on relationships to get things done.	a) has trouble with new jobs, situations, people (too ambiguous) b) gets irritated easily when things don't go right c) not developing a strategic perspective d) doesn't adapt to new cultures or changes well e) hasn't made a transition to an unknown area	Giving up old ways of doing things essential to succeed at more complex assignments	Can't make transition to more strategic, complex roles

4. Creative, conceptually strong, ball of fire, finger in many pies.	a) lack of attention to essential detail b) disorganization c) speedboats along; leaves people dangling d) hasn't really completed an assignment in depth	Depth, nitty-gritty required as well as awareness of how one is perceived if one doesn't follow through on commitments/details	Lacks follow-through (ie., can't be trusted to perform)
5. Has a single notable characteristic, such as tons of energy, raw talent or a long-term mentor.	a) too many eggs in one basket b) staying with same person too long c) hasn't stood alone	Increasing complexity requires broader skills repertoire, standing on one's own without a shield (talent, supportive boss)	Overdependence on . . . single strength
6. Contentious, loves to argue, takes strong stands, usually right.	a) doesn't know how to sell a position, cajole b) has to win c) trouble adapting to those with different styles	Cajoling, persuasion, understanding of group process required	Strategic differences with upper management; can't influence across dotted lines

The stakes change as well. Early career managers supervise small groups of professionals, often have supportive bosses who show them the ropes, and serve as project members. They rarely start business units from scratch, get thrown into massive operations they know little about, or get asked to turn around broken and bleeding business units (Lindsey, Homes, & McCall, 1987).[†] Tolerance for mistakes and lack of management flexibility decrease dramatically as the stakes change, the costs soar, and standards shift. "Suddenly":

- A strength no longer matters (i.e., managing a small professional group).

- A strength becomes a weakness ("She controls things" becomes "She sits on people and tries to do everything herself").

- An untested area becomes a weakness ("He never had to think strategically before and once it was required, he didn't seem to know how").

- A flaw now matters ("She never could build a team, but it wasn't critical").

- A blind spot becomes a flaw ("He viewed his arrogance as high standards and eventually ran out of people to work with").

Those who derail cling to past habits for at least two reasons. They like to do things their way, which is to rely on their greatest strengths, and they have been visibly rewarded for doing things their way. Over time, they slide into trouble for what they don't do, which is to change their management behavior in response to different demands and different people.

To illustrate the process of derailment we introduce Michelle, a high-potential manager. Using the derailment checklist (p. 11), we invite you to look at her as a potential derailer. Keeping in mind that both successful and derailed managers have flaws, you should check only notable flaws.

[†] Average age managers encounter certain experiences: First Management Job, 24; Project Task Force, 34; Start from Scratch, 38; Turnaround, Large Jump in Scope, 39.

Derailment Checklist

Michelle

___ 1. Doesn't develop subordinates.

___ 2. Doesn't resolve conflict among or with subordinates.

___ 3. Poor delegator—likes to do it alone.

___ 4. Gets irritated easily, especially with those seen as less able.

___ 5. Has trouble in *new* situations (over-relies on self or technical skills).

___ 6. Is a hands-on manager to a fault.

___ 7. Lacks attention to essential detail.

___ 8. Things slip through the cracks often.

___ 9. Involved in too much.

___ 10. Seen as very ambitious—overly interested in the next job.

___ 11. Abrasive.

___ 12. Makes others feel stupid or diminished.

___ 13. Volatile under pressure.

___ 14. Doesn't get the most out of people.

___ 15. Leaves people dangling due to unmet promises.

___ 16. Has stayed with the same person (mentor, boss) too long.

___ 17. Over-relies on core talent (e.g., energy, brains, good with subordinates).

___ 18. Doesn't sell/cajole well.

___ 19. Has to win.

___ 20. Has trouble adapting to those with different style.

Derailment: The Individual Face

Michelle was pistol-direct, aggressive, competitive, and bright. She had an MBA from a good university and had completed two high-quality internships—one with a financial services company and one with a competitor of her current company.

Quickly rotating through a number of assignments in corporate finance, she first attracted the attention of the Chief Financial Officer, Jack, when he attended presentations she gave on various projects. Quite willing to debate anyone, she often disagreed with higher management. She was equally outspoken with her peers and didn't mind showing off her considerable analytic skills.

Personally, she was delightfully funny, enjoyed jokes, and often held parties and dinners at her home. She was a superb, gracious hostess. In team meetings, she was argumentative and aggressive but polite. She prefaced remarks with, "I think" or "Another way to look at this is . . . ." She was tactful, even when rejecting a notion she may have thought silly.

One of her earlier bosses said of her: "She gives people a chance to undumb themselves—she asks lots of questions, gives careful feedback, delegates complete tasks with careful instructions. And on top of her brilliance and competence, she's genuinely funny."

Because of her obvious skills, Michelle was given a number of "first" assignments: first woman on the Capital Expenditures Committee, even though her level and position didn't match that of the other members; first woman on the cross-function visit and learn program where fast-trackers spent two weeks a quarter working with peers in other functions; and first woman in the Chairman's Club, another fast-track group who met for a series of four breakfasts with the Chairman.

The combination of these factors both helped and hurt her. She was visible and made a strong impression on everyone, but her reputation was far better with bosses ("Bright; courageous") than with peers and subordinates ("I just don't like to work with her"). Moving quickly also helped and hurt. Her broad exposure in only three years—planning, treasury, tax, audit, consolidation, technical control and analysis—increased her technical acumen, yet the speed with which she was moved and the typically flat financial structure (two or three levels) left her with little chance to supervise or get feedback. Her one supervisory job had lasted just 10 months, and although her group manager heard grumbling about her as a manager, she had left prior to appraisal time. In her management role, she had gotten along with others well, but also gained a reputation for being controlling and doing too much of the work herself.

This view hadn't spread very far, and at the next people review session three or four controllers in the line business units asked for her (a rare consensus event) and Jack, the CFO, decided to move her to the unit with the largest finance group to aid in her growth. Such a move was without precedent. Michelle knew next to nothing about the business, yet due to strong endorsement from senior management, she was put in charge of the business unit's planning group of five.

Michelle attacked the job—got right on a plane and made a field tour, worked in a plant, rode with several salespeople, worked at a distribution center and a warehouse, and came back and met with her subordinates. Armed with fresh field data and a sound understanding of the unit's business plan, Michelle questioned and pushed. Some were amused, some pleased, and some intimidated. She detected some flaws and new opportunities in the current year's plan and started selling.

Michelle's move into planning for the next year produced a plan in the shortest time ever. She also worked closely with her five subordinates, keeping them fully informed and giving carefully detailed feedback on every task they did. Because they all worked late, she often treated the team to pizza.

The person she replaced, Tom, moved on to be the controller of another unit. Tom was a good people manager who had personally assembled four of the five people now working for Michelle. With his legacy still fresh and although they liked her, they all reacted negatively to Michelle's style of managing. In their view, they were less involved, were doing lower level work, and knew less about what was going on than before. In addition, they all felt they had no career champion because she spent little time with them on anything but the day's work and social chatter.

Because they felt her joking nature reflected a need to distance herself, to cover up her lack of concern for them with jokes and dinner, her team didn't feel comfortable going to her with their concerns, and a few went to Tom. He listened to them and agreed to alert Michelle.

It was a memorable exchange. She had just received positive feedback from above about the plan and was "feeling her oats." Tom started by saying there were some things he thought she ought to know about how her team felt about her. After listening to him for a few minutes, Michelle's native aggressiveness surfaced and she exploded: called Tom a "wimpy" manager, said the team got used to low standards under him, cited her superior performance on the plan, told Tom to stay out of her business and added she wasn't sure any of "his" people were good enough to survive anyway. Tom, uncharacteristically, countered with some sexist language and questioned whether *she* was going to survive. Michelle ended the conversation by replying that he was the one who wouldn't make it.

In the meantime her boss, Jim, the business unit controller, and Mike, the GM, began to hear the noise from her team. Mike was very pleased with her work but asked Jim to talk to her about being more sensitive to the needs of the team.

Unaware of the confrontation with Tom, Jim chose that same afternoon to give Michelle feedback on not being a team player. He was surprised at the intensity of Michelle's reaction to what he considered to be a minor issue. She said she was sick and tired of unqualified people telling her how she ought to act and added that all this "style stuff" was just the "old-boy" network doing its thing to hold women from breaking through the "glass ceiling." She then countered that Mike didn't have a problem with her style, and when Jim told her that Mike had asked him to talk to her, she ended by saying that since performance didn't count in this company, she might as well leave.

By the next day, the full story came together as Tom and Jim talked with each other. Meanwhile, Michelle had holed up in her office and had cancelled most of her schedule. There was a real risk of losing her. She frequently received search calls.

If you wish, stop here and complete the derailment checklist on page 11 for Michelle before turning the page to see which problems we checked.

Michelle is a typical candidate for later derailment: a bright, driven person who has developed her individual skills at the expense of others.

1. A strength masks a weakness or weaknesses: her technical skills and good judgment produce results, but she has significant problems managing.

2. Untested areas will cripple her eventually. She has little notion of making the transition to a more strategic perspective, building a team, or learning to lose and fight another day.

3. She has a blind spot that will eventually matter. Stars get a lot of *what* (accomplishments) feedback but less *how* (method and style)

feedback. She doesn't really know how she is viewed by others and they have not been as helpful as they could have been.

These three forces—strengths masking weaknesses, ignorance of untested areas, and being visibly rewarded for glowing results—further blind her to herself, helping make her appear arrogant. She is not open to hearing the bad news.

So what can be done to help Michelle, to prevent her possible derailment? First, we will return to what happened with Michelle, then explore the principles behind what happened.

Michelle

Jim (her boss), Mike (GM), Jack (CFO), and Marv (the Director of Management Development) had a hurry-up meeting. All agreed that Michelle was talented but that her impact on her subordinates was a potential "fatal" flaw.

Jack and Marv were seen as sufficiently remote from the battle, but credible enough to deliver some messages: (1) Everyone wanted her to stay, (2) Nobody's perfect and that's okay, (3) She needed to make some transitions and many were willing to help, and (4) Her future was still bright.

After Jim asked Tom to stay away from Michelle for a while, Jack met with her to let her vent. The same themes arose. Performance didn't matter. The glass ceiling for women. Style shouldn't matter. Most others were incompetent. Double standard. All her hard work didn't count. Tom's weak. She asked Jack whether he thought she should quit and find a company where her real skills would be valued.

Jack delivered the messages. They all accepted her as she was and believed she had a strong career ahead of her. Nobody's perfect, including her. They wanted her to pause and listen before she did anything. He shared some personal traumas he had as a first-time manager, not too dissimilar from Michelle's issues, and assured her that the "damage," as she called it, could be handled with her people, the business unit, and with Tom. He suggested she meet with Marv to verify her standing and she agreed.

When they met the next day, Michelle was somewhat more positive after the strong support voiced by Jack. Marv repeated the messages and Michelle said she'd listen.

Derailment Checklist

Michelle

___ 1. Doesn't develop subordinates.

___ 2. Doesn't resolve conflict among or with subordinates.

_X_ 3. Poor delegator—likes to do it alone.

___ 4. Gets irritated easily, especially with those seen as less able.

___ 5. Has trouble in *new* situations (over-relies on self or technical skills).

___ 6. Is a hands-on manager to a fault.

___ 7. Lacks attention to essential detail.

___ 8. Things slip through the cracks often.

___ 9. Involved in too much.

___ 10. Seen as very ambitious—overly interested in the next job.

___ 11. Abrasive.

_X_ 12. Makes others feel stupid or diminished.

_X_ 13. Volatile under pressure.

_X_ 14. Doesn't get the most out of people.

___ 15. Leaves people dangling due to unmet promises.

___ 16. Has stayed with the same person (mentor, boss) too long.

_X_ 17. Over-relies on core talent (e.g., energy, brains, good with subordinates).

___ 18. Doesn't sell/cajole well.

_X_ 19. Has to win.

___ 20. Has trouble adapting to those with different style.

First, Marv reviewed the research on why talented managers derail, common management transitions, and the key lessons successful executives needed to learn. They discussed her strengths and needs in that context. Then to lock in the data, he suggested getting more formal feedback from others via a Management Practices Questionnaire. She agreed and picked the people.

The data was as he expected. Bosses positive, peers mixed, and subordinates (past and present) negative. Her self-appraisal agreed mostly with the bosses. As they worked through the data, Marv pinpointed (1) regard for others judged mostly on intelligence and degree of directness and (2) low tolerance for due process (defined as any way of doing things other than Michelle's) as the prime drivers resulting in poor team-building and delegating skills.

Michelle bristled. "How can they say that? I'm nice to everyone—I involve everyone. That's team-playing."

"Michelle," Marv said, "your impact on other people is sometimes more what you don't do than what you do." From conversations with many co-workers, Marv had pieced together why people reacted to her as they did. Slowly he began to paint another portrait for her.

While Michelle certainly was polite, likeable, and involved everyone, her involvement was of the "Let's discuss my view of the problem" variety. She solicited input, but rarely opinions. She never sat a group down and said, "This and this are happening. What do you think the problem is?" She rarely asked for help but she often asked for tasks to be done to help her. "I'm sure she's stumped as often as anyone else, but she'd never say so," one subordinate said.

Although she gave careful, helpful feedback, her feedback ran from neutral to critical. She never said, "This part is terrific, I learned this and this from your analysis" or "I like the way you conceptualized this." Good meant it fit the way Michelle wanted it; bad meant any deviation from her method and all deviations were to be gently corrected.

Overall, Michelle affected people in the following ways. They admired her brilliance and her wit and liked to go play with her. But her opinion of others was revealed by what she didn't do. As one subordinate told Marv, "Finally you realize you've been run over by a velvet steam roller. After a few months it dawns on you that she's never asked about your career or for your help in defining problems; that while she listens politely and responds tactfully, nothing happens as a result of your ideas. What you get is feedback on how you failed to measure up to her standards and then it hits you: She's never once said she liked anything that you initiated. She thinks you're sort of stupid and she's humoring you through her jokes. That's when I realized what I am to her: I'm Michelle's pencil."

Michelle, who thought of herself as approachable and bright, was floored by the idea that she used people as pencils. Marv shifted gears, emphasizing that no one questioned her intentions. It was her methods that caused her problems, and methods could be changed. Although what he said wasn't entirely candid, Michelle was reeling and he didn't want to help tip her over. First, Marv wanted to prop her ego up a bit and help her put her problems in context. Second, he wanted to add some team-building skills to Michelle's analytic skills so she wouldn't fall back on doing everything herself under stress.

Over the next month, Marv first helped Michelle sort through her problems. They discussed some of the forces that acted on her as a woman and as a manager, and talked through her feelings about the double standard and the pressure on her being "first" onstage. Marv gave her some reading materials to become more familiar with the demands placed on managers and how managers could "suddenly" derail. What Marv hoped Michelle would see was that the pressures of being "first" were exacerbating her problem. The more pressure she felt to perform, the more she overrelied on her analytical strengths and turned them into a weakness.

Their discussion and her reading helped Michelle feel less alone. One day she said to Marv, "I see now that I'm not some sort of uncaring manipulator. I feel heat, I fall back on my strengths, I forget to do other things, and what I don't do gets me in trouble. But we all do this at times—our strengths can do us in as easily as our weaknesses."

Second, Marv had Michelle attend two executive skills workshops. One was "Developing Leaders for Tomorrow"—a course reviewing the tools and techniques for helping others grow. When they debriefed after the workshop, Michelle agreed she was pretty far away from being a developmental supervisor, one step forward for her. The other course was "Understanding How a Company Works"—a course designed to show how to get things done in a complex organization and how due process plays out for everyone's long-term benefit. Again, Michelle admitted her view of how things worked didn't match.

Up to this point, Michelle was dealing with her insights mechanically. To be a better manager, she needed to engage in certain specified behaviors. But she neither owned the behaviors nor really understood how she devalued others. For Michelle to understand, she needed to delve below the surface and realize that she devalued those who failed to reflect her image of what mattered in life—to be bright and direct. Marv's experience told him that without this realization, Michelle would revert to her old ways under stress. Marv said, "Let's pick some people we both know well and independently put them into two imaginary buckets. The bright and direct go in the first bucket and the not so bright and political go in the second bucket." Once they did, Michelle was surprised that their separation into buckets was virtually identical. "The problem isn't your judgment, Michelle," Marv said, "it's your dealings with the less bright and less direct." He told her she needed to learn to find more value in the "bad" bucket people, and not to signal to them what bucket they were in. After all, few people were as bright as Michelle, so the "bad" bucket would always be full; but this was not to say that they didn't have other gifts, gifts that perhaps she lacked. "So maybe you should quit thinking of people in buckets, maybe that's not as useful as figuring out what their gifts are."

This seemed to bring on Michelle's moment of truth. Like any aha!, it was the result of trying many variations on a theme until something clicks. For Michelle, the buckets exercise lit a light for her. She began to own up to the issues. She realized there was more to effectiveness at work than her narrow test. She made peace with Tom who apologized as well. Jim (her boss) and Mike (the GM) took over the development process with the on-the-job coaching.

Based on Marv's suggestions, Jim and Mike focused on three strategies: they empathized with Michelle on how hard it is to grit your teeth and do things that go against the grain, they gave her simple behavioral strategies for doing so, and they set up numerous practice settings.

Slowly, she began to modify her behavior. She jointly defined problems, gave positive feedback, and admitted occasionally that she was stumped or didn't know something. She held more staff meetings, had personal updates and development talks with her people, worked on inclusion with peers, and tried to be more open to others' ideas. She even gave up on having to win every battle.

Jim and Mike did not let early success lull them into letting up. Both gave her repeated feedback on how she came across in meetings, asking her to critique her performance and occasionally suggesting other tactics. They also invented small project assignments with peers where Michelle was not in charge and had to rely on persuasion. Finally, they placed her on a product roll-out task force to give her a taste of what it felt like to know much less than the other task force members.

As Michelle progressed, Marv reentered to troubleshoot two complications. The first was that some people were suspicious of the "new" Michelle; the second was that Michelle still lacked a rationale for what she was doing. She engaged in piecemeal behaviors that occasionally rang hollow.

Through asking questions, Marv helped Michelle pinpoint what she needed to do, which was to develop some specific rules of thumb. She decided to level with each of her co-workers about her intentions and ask for their help in changing. To this point, she had stubbornly refused to explain her actions, naively believing that people would "just accept that I've changed." She also decided to alter her method of giving and receiving feedback and how she delegated tasks.

Following is a partial list of the rules of thumb she and Marv derived:

1. Level about my intentions and ask for help.

2. When giving feedback, divide it into three chunks: What I liked, meaning here's how you influenced my thinking; what I think is arguable—let's discuss it; where I think you're wrong or, at the least, I can't follow your reasoning.

3. When delegating, discuss the entire conceptual area, not just the specific task. Talk about how to think this through in collaboration with subordinates.

4. When I draw a conclusion, take the time to explain how I got there. Extend others the same courtesy, rather than immediately evaluating the conclusion.

5. Figure out what everyone's greatest strength is and show appreciation for it. Give candid feedback on where they can improve.

Marv helped Michelle to guard against the pendulum swings that often retard development. Occasionally when confronted with what she thought was a bad notion, she would freeze and mumble "Let's try it" because she feared criticism; at other times, she would be blandly positive, retreating into smiles or "Yes"–"No" commentaries instead of engaging the issues and revealing her thought process.

Marv wanted Michelle to realize that her best bet was to use her greatest strength to attack her weaknesses. She was bright and analytical so he wanted her to analyze her behavior as she would analyze a task. Further, he wanted her to share her greatest gift—her thought processes—with others. Perhaps without knowing it, she might influence how others thought and be influenced as well. With more listening going on inside, Marv hoped that Michelle might learn a few things about how to think herself, particularly about how to take others' needs into account. Who knew? Someday, someone might even refer to her as a patient person.

Again, Marv asked Michelle to do some reading, this time about the process of behavioral change. The major point he hoped she'd note was that she would only succeed if she deployed her strengths well. Either underdoing or overdoing them was equally damaging.

Michelle got the message, realizing that she had been acting a bit on and off and that a third way was both possible and desirable. Rules of thumb in hand, she returned to her team.

At this date, Michelle is performing better and remains on the high-potential list. While she may never become a disciple of participative management, she no longer makes others feel like pencils.

Developing Michelle

There are four general principles of individual management development (broken into 12 steps on page 22), applied here to the special case of derailers:

1. Preparing managers for change by showing a realistic picture of themselves;

2. Transferring the information to personal ownership so managers feel responsible for their development;

3. Developing managers through a series of targeted tactics; and

4. Rewarding managers for improvement.

Preparing. First, Michelle had to be presented with a standard to measure herself against—a depiction of what effectiveness and derailment look like and the dynamic transitions necessary as managerial careers ad-

Principles of Management Development

PRINCIPLES	STEP	QUESTIONS
PREPARING	1 Targeting	Do you know what set of skills and competencies is/will be needed? Do you know what leads to derailment?
	2 Observing/ Documenting	Have you adequately observed and documented behavior and performance on each critical skill and competency?
	3 Evaluating	Do you know where they stand on each skill and competency?
TRANSFER-RING	4 Becoming Aware	Are they aware others think they have the need?
	5 Taking Ownership	Do they personally buy into and accept the need as theirs?
	6 Understanding the Consequences	Do they understand how this need impacts current performance and/or affects their future and goals important to them?
	7 Becoming a Stakeholder	Are they motivated to work on the need?
DEVELOPING	8 Visioning the Outcome	Do they know what the outcome looks like? Do they know the end result of the effort?
	9 Building and Developing	Do they have the insights and skills required to address the need without outside assistance and/or has a planned development effort been applied to address the need?
	10 Practicing and Re-entry	Has adequate opportunity to apply/practice the acquired knowledge, skill, or trait and/or attitude been provided? Has re-entry been planned and managed?
LOCK-IN	11 Demonstrating Mastery	Can they fully and completely perform and exhibit the acquired knowledge, skill and/or attitude? Is the need gone?
	12 Rewarding the Effort	Has adequate feedback and support been given? Have the rewards promised in #6 been delivered?

vance (Marv had to piece this together himself; their organization didn't have such a profile). The three preparing steps involve taking a realistic profile and locating people on it behaviorally. In Michelle's case, she needed to see how her behavior hurt her as a manager. So the first developmental principle is to collect information to show a person the impact of their behaviors on an effectiveness and derailment profile. Nothing changes reliably without a target or standard to be measured against.

Transferring. The second principle is to transfer the information to ownership, which triggers the motivation to develop. "Stars" in trouble are as resistant as anyone else to bad news. Indeed, because they have been singled out as special, they are sometimes more resistant, virtually immune to corrective feedback: Their most typical responses are "It's not an accurate assessment" or "It's other people's fault" or to deny that their "flaws" have any impact. Pressure must be applied through repeated information-giving tactics to counter the resistance of those who fail to see how changing expectations are altering others' views of their strengths and weaknesses. Michelle believed that analytical problem solving and direct influence were her greatest strengths. She had been rewarded for them and thought that others were just jealous. She had to be gently led to see that there was more to management than this, that other skills were important, and that across time, new strengths would become more important. Like Scrooge, she needed a look into the future.

We have found the best information transfer tactic is 360-degree feedback[†] on a behaviorally based managerial practices questionnaire. This should be completed by all relevant groups of people. In addition, selected workshops also heighten awareness. Even for Michelles, it is difficult to ignore what many others are concluding about you.

Beyond these tactics, patience and lots of caring conversations are necessary. We emphasize talking because it's critical that potential derailers have one or more people to turn to and that they not be expected or allowed to work out of the hole by themselves. Conversations with someone other than a boss are critical to preserving the person's core values and sense of competency while attempting to create new needs in the person. So the second developmental principle is to help the person perceive the truth from as many credible sources as possible. It's especially difficult for super successful young people to see their dark sides.

[†] 360-degree feedback—from bosses, self, peers, clients, subordinates, significant others.

Developing. Once ownership is achieved, what works best is to use the person's greatest strengths to address the needs. Michelle was a problem solver, given the challenge of solving her greatest problem to date. Once she understood the consequences of her behavior, she quickly saw what new behavior would help her, and was motivated to apply her strong problem-solving skills to the change effort.

Actual development (Step 9) is in the hands of the person, but they can't do it themselves because few understand what experiences and learning tactics are most likely to be effective.

The Center for Creative Leadership studies of learning from experience showed that the first management job is overwhelmingly a time for building basic lessons: that management is different from technical work—that knowing the right answer isn't enough, that cajoling and team-building are equally important in getting things done. These lessons apparently must be learned. There was evidence that whenever those who went on to be successful encountered their first management job—at 23 or at 40—they learned these somewhat primitive lessons. This was virtually the only developmental job in which a supportive boss/mentor played a major role (the others were characterized by going it alone). So ideally, the first supervisory job is a moderately safe time to learn, practice, and develop one's basic managerial skills (McCall et al., 1988).

It was decided that Michelle could work on her issues in her present job, with coursework and temporary mentoring being pivotal. Courses, feedback, and education about the management/organization world to open her eyes to what a developmental supervisor looked like along with straight but kindly advice from mentors was necessary to help her beyond her defensiveness and lack of knowledge. To throw her into a new assignment would probably have derailed her.

Michelle's boss, Jim, had powerful roles in her development—such as coaching and documenting her progress against the model. But a sometimes often overlooked role was also important: serving as a values monitor. Michelle didn't really understand how her actions lead to value-laden conclusions by others (she thought she was problem solving; others felt devalued and stupid). It was Jim's job to make sure she understood how her small, day-to-day actions had a huge values impact. Through repeated feedback sessions and conversations, Michelle developed more empathy and more ability to have the kind of impact she wanted without the damage of her old ways.

While still on her present job, Michelle was given additional tests— projects where she had to persuade, even one where she knew little about the task. Each assignment was selected to teach and reinforce new skills and to induce a little humility as a prelude to her appreciating the skills that others have. If Michelle had been two levels higher at the point where she ran into trouble, the stakes might have changed enough that she would have had to demonstrate that she could perform in a new job.

In this event we have found it best to have carefully selected job assignments that naturally emphasize a specific developmental challenge; in her case, involving and persuading rather than going it alone. During the rebuilding period, she would be moved through multiple special assignments, all aimed at neutralizing her weaknesses and teaching new skills: managing a project where she was not expert and the subordinates were; managing a system installation where she had no authority over those installing the system; or working for a boss who excelled at persuasion.

The tactic of targeted multiple assignments is one developmental key to preventing derailment. Without repeated reminders in different situations, potential derailers will usually revert to their greatest strength (which is becoming a weakness). After all, the strength carried them this far and learning a new strength, particularly one like persuasion and appreciation of others, takes some time.

The final key was Marv's role. Beginning with basic information on her performance, he slowly asked Michelle to confront her underlying problems and make gradual changes. To ask her initially to drop her present "model" and adopt her eventual "model," in our experience, does not work. The change is too huge and too threatening. Marv fed her what he thought she could handle so she could learn bit by bit, on the job.

The third principle of management development is that the person confront their biggest development need on the job. The tactics may vary markedly according to the managerial experience of the person. For Michelle, the process was heavily educational with practice on her present job; if she had been more experienced, she might have had to prove herself in different arenas.

Rewarding. Finally, Michelle had to be rewarded for her efforts in order for the change to stick. Careful development and continued feedback resulted in her remaining firmly on the high-potential track. She clearly saw how her efforts led to both intrinsic and extrinsic rewards. So the fourth developmental principle is the law of cause and effect. Michelle had to clearly see how her behavioral changes made a difference.

The process works similarly with other types of potential derailers. They must be led to a broader conception of management, take ownership of how they stack up against this conception (represented by an effectiveness/derailment profile), and be rewarded for their behavioral changes. The specific developmental efforts will be different, of course. A narrow, technical manager might be asked to go through a series of strategic planning assignments; a manager who works with a well-functioning group might be placed with problem groups; a creative manager with fingers in many pies might be forced to focus on one pie and follow through on each task and all essential detail. Regardless, the purposes are the same—to overcome or minimize weaknesses and to develop more of the attributes demanded of today's leaders: adaptability in the face of a variety of challenges; recognition of interdependencies and the need to build teams in a variety of settings with a variety of beliefs and motives; and heightened self-awareness and concern for others.

In summary, individual management development is governed by four principles: (1) locating the person on a realistic effectiveness/derailment profile, (2) helping the person take ownership of his or her impact through 360-degree feedback, (3) choosing on-the-job developmental practices that are specific to the person's needs, and (4) visibly rewarding the person for behavioral changes.

But What About Sexism?

Doesn't it make a difference that Michelle is a woman? The answers are no and yes.

The No's

1. No responsible study of management (see Bray & Howard, 1988; Bentz, 1986, for example) has detected any skill differences between men and women, nor any difference in what skills are necessary for effectiveness.

2. Michelle is at an earlier phase in her career. The difference in her developmental plan holds for everyone at that phase. CCL's women executives study (Morrison, White, & Van Velsor, 1987) showed how moving women prematurely set them up for derailment. (The same, of course, holds true for men.)

3. Organizations inadvertently create derailers by moving managers too fast or too slowly, by sticking them in a series of low challenge jobs, or by placing on the fast track and rewarding those who are likely to get in trouble as expectations change.

The Yes's

1. Derailment factors for men and women are basically the same, but for women certain factors are more pronounced: Being seen as overly ambitious, handling performance problems poorly and failure to lead subordinates well were much more frequent for women. All of these have the ring of a double standard to them, particularly when even successful women executives were *three* times less likely to have had the major developmental assignments that season managers most: starting something from scratch, fixing a broken unit, or having a large jump in scope (moving into a complex, well-functioning operation) (Morrison et al., 1987).

   Learning how to handle performance problems and lead subordinates usually occur during developmental job assignments women are less likely to have had. Overambition for women might be sexism ("She's too pushy") or perhaps just the unfamiliarity of men with the female version of the male ambition.

   So derailment factors for women, while similar, appear to have a bit of a self-fulfilling prophecy to them. Many women enter in peripheral low-challenge staff roles, are further protected by paternalism or victimized by discrimination, and hardly surprisingly end up perceived as managers who are lacking in basic supervisory skills.

2. Women *may* have to perform better than men to get ahead. Sometimes that's the only way for out-group members to get credibility with the in-group. Research at AT&T's third-level assessment center indicates there may be some validity to this claim: among women and men at the same levels, women had higher assessed skills (Bunker, 1987).

Derailment: The Organizational Face

Managers often derail themselves. In addition, they need to look over their shoulders since organizations derail them as well with the following formal or de facto "developmental" processes and beliefs:

1. Defining development largely as educational experiences and job rotations when this is only 8% of what executives mention (Lindsey et al., 1987).

2. Moving people so fast they never really finish a job. Like one executive said, "I've always had time to fix it but not to have my mistakes catch up with me. I imagine someday they will." Conversely, some organizations move people so slowly that they master the job and begin to get very bored. (See Gabarro, 1987, for a discussion of time in job.)

3. Considering vertical movement in one area a meaningful developmental sequence. On the contrary, this tends to stick people in a series of low-challenge jobs or the same jobs over and over. A common pattern among derailers is to go straight up in operations that are doing at least adequately well. Regardless of their other merits, from a leadership challenge point of view, these small vertical jumps are basically more of the same.

4. Having one failure knock someone off the fast track, when 15% of successful executives volunteered that they derailed (McCall et al., 1988). There was a trend in the CCL studies for successful managers to report more failures and mistakes. After all, future leaders are supposed to be curious, calculated risk-taker types. One former CEO gives a deadpan speech warning young managers of the three biggest mistakes they can make by illustrating them with blunders from his own career.

5. Loading up the fast track with aggressive, arrogant, independent types who run into trouble later as strengths become liabilities. Early they're often seen as hard-driving and results-oriented, later they're often seen as sitting on people, poor team-builders or non-strategic.

6. Giving lots of results of "what you did" feedback, but little "how you did it" feedback. Studies (DeVries, Morrison, Shullman, & Gerlach, 1981; Kaplan, Drath, & Kofodimos, 1985) indicate that fast-track managers are less likely to get "how" developmental feedback—they typically move fast and work for bosses who also move fast. I'm sure all of us have spoken with managers who got their first "how you did it" feedback when they derailed.

7. Our achievement-oriented society and compensation systems equate success with moving up instead of moving around to confront new leadership challenges. All the developmental jobs executives cited were tough challenges; only some were promotions, making effective career paths in reality a zigzag instead of a vertical arrow.

8. Confusing basic intelligence, technical and functional expertise with the ability to learn new patterns from experience when these are not the same attribute. In studies at Florida State and Yale, what Wagner and Sternberg call "street smarts" is most related to various measures of actual performance and "street smarts" is unrelated to measures of intelligence. Many organizations hire on grade point average, which can be predicted fairly well from intelligence tests but which doesn't predict actual performance well. To the extent that organizations ignore "street smarts"—the ability to use one's intelligence in practical situations—they may select and develop the wrong people (Wagner & Sternberg, 1985, 1987).

Many entry-level managers and professionals are quite naive. They have little notion of leadership or how organizations actually work. For example, in some of John Kotter's work at the Harvard Business School with MBA students—90% of whom had business experience—46% were judged to be naive in their assessment of a complex business case (Kotter, 1985).

Many bump along, piling up technical and functional knowledge, trying to get promoted, but gaining their leadership perspective by chance. Without help, many talented people end up narrow in experience, indifferent learners where leadership perspective is concerned, with only hit or miss feedback to guide them. Such people—who are numerous, not few—often get into trouble or actually derail; and when they do, few organizations relish the confrontations necessary to clear the air. The sad truth is that many Michelles would go on to derail.

In contrast, the CCL studies found that some combination of three differences distinguished successful from derailed executives:

- They gleaned useful feedback on their performance, largely from reflecting on their successes and failures on the job.

- They had greater variety in the leadership challenges they faced.

- They were, or were helped to be, avid learners of new management behavior which could lead to more of a balanced perspective (McCall et al., 1988).

Following is a depiction of what organizations can do to prevent derailment by more actively managing the development of their managers. We will discuss three topics, which are further subdivided into eight recommendations: getting quality feedback to managers on an effectiveness and derailment profile; increasing the variety of experience for managers; and creating a more active learning environment for managers.

Feedback on an Effectiveness and Derailment Profile

Many organizations have armchair effectiveness profiles (meaning what attributes top managers think they possess or ought to possess), a few have data-based ones, but only a smattering have derailment profiles. In our experience working with these profiles, many are flawed in at least some of the following ways: too much emphasis on technical/functional knowledge, too many murky terms like vision and aggressiveness, too limited a notion of what effectiveness is, and no measurement of flaws.

Recommendation 1. Develop a data-based behavioral effectiveness and derailment profile. The mechanics of this are beyond the scope of a discussion of preventing derailment, so we will restrict the discussion to essentials.

First—given the nature of the business, organizational and personal demands faced now and into the foreseeable future—ask groups of managers what leadership challenges they face in order to meet these demands. If this is too difficult, managers might begin with major challenges they have faced in the past few years—a particularly challenging job, an excellent or difficult boss, a mistake they made or inherited. (Coping with each of these was cited by executives as having a major impact on their development.) The point is to get managers talking about real challenges and real experiences, rather than abstractions, so they can discuss what must be done to meet these challenges.

Second, the behaviors necessary for effectiveness should be categorized. In our experience, five factors tend to emerge, two specific to the organization and three more general. The first is the specific technical/functional/business knowledges required; the second are cultural norms around what is acceptable behavior within each organization. The other three are some variation of the factors found in Center for Creative Leadership research: adaptability in a variety of leadership settings, team-building/understanding other peoples' needs, and the personal effectiveness factor of self-awareness and tolerance for others.

Third, what gets managers into serious trouble? The flaws that can override strengths tend to be those defined on page 6, but we have found that each organization has different wrinkles and sometimes a dramatically different emphasis resulting from their selection and socialization practices (e.g., some organizations rarely have people derail for interpersonal problems because they put a premium on such skills in selection and socialization).

Fourth, the profile should be looked at very carefully to see if it will hold up in the future tense. We find, for example, that some profiles do not fully take into account the need for quick innovation and sensitivity to many different groups of people demanded by the increases in interdependence and the sheer complexity of leadership in the last 20 or 30 years.

Fifth, the profile should be stated in behavioral terms. What would a person do to demonstrate adaptability, for example? There are many instruments available that state effectiveness factors behaviorally so a manager can understand what is needed. A commercially available instrument amended to include organizationally specific knowledge and behavior can be helpful here, so each organization does not have to reinvent the wheel. We do want to emphasize that organizations should decide what to measure first to get an inclusive view, then see what help is available.

The essence of this recommendation is to give all managers a believable target, one that acknowledges that we have flaws as well as strengths, and that if our flaws are serious ones they must be addressed before, like Michelle, they may override any number of strengths.

In addition, the CCL studies and others have provided little support for the notion that future executives get much developmental feedback or race around eagerly seeking feedback from others. High-potential managers get *less* feedback than managers in trouble, often do not have formal performance appraisals (DeVries et al., 1981), and usually prefer to get feedback from success or failure on *tasks*. They are likely to be independent and achievement-oriented (Bray & Howard, 1988), both of which influence them to rely on task feedback and either be disinterested or simply not think about detailed feedback from others. Single-source learners like Michelle can easily slide into trouble without the organization intervening to help.

Recommendation 2. Make the profile widely known through providing both a rationale for it and 360-degree feedback for all managers. First, provide career information for all young managers. An excellent mechanism for doing this is to have informal sessions where young managers hear seasoned executives talk about the key events in their careers—challenging jobs they faced, important other people they encountered, their blunders, timely courses, and feedback. Such sessions are eye openers for organizational rookies because they explain the nature of leadership: that leaders transition from one type of challenge to another, that present skills won't matter as much later, that new skills are needed, and that dark sides will eventually find a spotlight.

Reading materials are also useful to combat naiveté. John Kotter in *The Leadership Factor* (1988) discusses how to develop managers more intelligently; Jack Gabarro in *The Dynamics of Taking Charge* (1987) details how to transition to a new job and all the mistakes managers are likely to make. Jim Kouzes and Barry Posner in *The Leadership Challenge* (1987) offer specific advice around how to behave in numerous management situations. Barbara Kovach follows 17 high-potential managers through success and derailment in *Survival on the Fast Track* (1988). The development of male and female executives is examined in *The Lessons of Experience* (McCall et al., 1988) and *Breaking the Glass Ceiling* (Morrison et al., 1987) from the Center for Creative Leadership.

Second, institute a 360-degree feedback program, preferably for all managers. An organization's ability to know who their high-potential managers are is not good. In fact, in the longitudinal AT&T studies, high assessed young managers were *29% less likely* to be promoted than lower assessed if the low assessed had higher subsequent job challenge, indicating that knowing who the future stars are is not an easy business (Bray, Campbell, & Grant, 1974). In the CCL studies, about 15% of successful executives volunteered that they had been derailed at one time (one was fired twice before he got the message; McCall et al., 1988). Even the best stumble, and the belief that the best will automatically learn what they need to learn is largely myth. All managers need feedback in order to grow, and organizations need 360-degree feedback to help determine who their high-potentials really are. Because development has long-term time frames, we have found that 360-degree feedback once every three years is sufficient.

Three hundred sixty degree feedback (boss, subordinates, and peers at a minimum, and colleagues in other units, customers, clients, boss's boss, and diagonal subordinates, if possible) is essential to give managers a complete picture of themselves. Each source has additional information. Peers often excel at feedback on persuasion, subordinates on motivational skills, and bosses on planning, strategy, and sizing up people; but according to studies, up to 90% of performance appraisals are given by the boss alone. Good bosses have always sought other feedback sources, of course, and some managers get 360-degree feedback through coursework, but this is a hit or miss practice not always geared toward leadership effectiveness for this manager at this time in this organization. Further, the majority of managers don't get 360-degree feedback at all.

Three hundred sixty degree feedback is also necessary because people show different faces to different people: Some excel with bosses and some with everyone but bosses; others can't deal with subordinates or peers but do well otherwise. It takes 360-degree feedback to uncover this easily. We might wonder if Michelle's boss during her first supervisory assignment had gotten feedback to her, if her development could have been less painful. As it was, she got a big promotion, had an incredible success with the next year's plan, then felt poleaxed. By the time Marv intervened, he had to piece together the story, then piece together a makeshift success and derailment profile using commercially available instruments and his home-grown measures. Marv and Michelle's organization had neither a success/derailment profile nor 360-degree feedback.

Three hundred sixty degree feedback has other benefits. It spreads the burden of giving bad news (few consider giving good news a burden), and is more credible to those who receive it. We have found that widespread 360-degree feedback systems help set a developmental climate throughout organizations: in general, people like to help others and be helped and it becomes okay, even encouraged, to give and receive constructive feedback. Delivered in a timely fashion, it helps break down the resistance that people often have to receive bad news.

Direct bosses needed to be trained in one-on-one coaching and counseling skills to help managers make sense of their feedback. Although the specifics of the feedback should be confidential, we encourage managers and bosses to discuss major issues. Bosses can also assist by telling selected stories about people who got ahead and people who derailed. A real presentation of good and bad consequences of developing or not developing helps move people to constructive action.

Recommendation 3. In the special case of potential derailers, bring in "inside outsiders." Diverting a potential derailer is a complicated process requiring many people that should be spearheaded by someone outside the chain of command—usually a human resources professional. It is essential when a situation has blown up or is about to, to bring in someone who knows the organization but who is not directly involved. As we have noted, potential derailers are usually extremely resistant to bad news because they've often been treated as stars or have failed to face up to a weakness until it becomes critical. Many discussions and special assignments, requiring the involvement of many people, will be necessary if this occurs, and an "inside outsider" is needed to orchestrate this.

Regardless of the particular combination, many future leaders have big strengths and corollary big weaknesses. Several studies suggest that not many people get to leadership roles by being "sort of good" at everything (Bass, 1985; Bray & Howard, 1988; McCall & Lombardo, 1983; McCall et al., 1988). They are great idea people or great at team-building, and with those strengths go things they dislike such as detail or abstraction. They also tend to be curious and like to try new things, so mistakes and outright messes may occur.

So, especially in the case of future leaders, derailment prevention may be necessary. If we take leadership literally, as a rare attribute, we need to accept that such people are a bit unusual too, that some will be like Michelle who in effect got into trouble for being a budding visionary; and like many visionaries, she wanted to do it herself and didn't "suffer fools gladly."

In the Center for Creative Leadership's derailment studies and other studies of key experiences and learning in the lives of executives, executives emphasized knowing strengths, concomitant weaknesses, and limits—things one has tried to do repeatedly and failed (see Bennis & Nanus, 1985). In derailment prevention for high-potentials, the issue becomes developing new strengths plus not letting one's weaknesses and limits do them in. Many future leaders are driven and aggressive and will need help before they cut themselves with their own rough edges.

In summary, feedback on a behaviorally-based effectiveness and derailment profile is necessary so young managers have a realistic viewpoint of what is expected and some help in development. Providing career information to "teach the ropes" and occasionally intervening to help talented but flawed managers is also recommended.

Increasing Variety of Experience for Managers

Challenging jobs teach about the subtleties of leadership—starting up or fixing troubled operations, expanding large operations, or working on time-limited projects, from crises to systems installations. Such jobs teach how to cope with pressure and ambiguity, learn quickly or deal with balky subordinates. In absolute terms, challenging assignments are the best teacher. They are most likely to be remembered as developmental, and can teach both the greatest variety and number of lessons.

Recommendation 4. Figure out what your challenging jobs are and why they're challenging. A simple practice used in some organizations is to interview small groups of managers in each major unit to get examples of their most challenging jobs. These are then written down as organizational examples of starting something from scratch or a turnaround and distributed with a clear message to seek variety in leadership challenge as well as learn the business, the function, and pick up needed technical skills. Other organizations use procedures such as designating key jobs, then analyzing their challenges. But whatever method is chosen, it's critical to know what your challenging jobs are so it is known what present and future leaders must face.

Recommendation 5. Save the best developmental jobs for high-potential managers. Obviously turnarounds and start-ups are not everyday occurrences and should be reserved for those who have the best chance of succeeding and learning from them.

Particularly for high-potential managers, invent ways to provide small challenges early. Organizations need to expose managers early to varied leadership challenges before the stakes get too high. By this we mean turning around a small unit in trouble, having to rely on persuasion to get things done, putting someone in a job where they can't possibly control every activity, starting something (a small unit, a procedure or process) from scratch, or learning to think strategically through a staff or project assignment.

Such small challenges are the breeding grounds of leaders because they can teach critical lessons. For example, many executives confront their first turnaround when the stakes are staggering, and failure is frequent. If a manager has never had to be simultaneously tough and compassionate, manage by remote control, confront problem subordinates, and build morale while tearing down inefficient systems and procedures (all required in a fix-it job), the chance of failure is heightened. Exposure to mini-versions of these challenges in early career allows time for learning via a strategy of small wins, small losses.

Again, Michelle could have been helped earlier with assignments where she wasn't the expert, such as task forces or volunteer work to improve her persuasiveness. She could have enhanced her feedback skills through coursework, training as an assessor in an assessment center, or having to teach someone something they didn't know how to do (e.g., teaching a child to read).

But some managers look good early and burn out; others bloom late. Without a constant focus on development in one's present job, many talented people will languish because they never had the chance. (Recall that in the AT&T studies, many "dogs" become "stars" once they had a challenge.)

Recommendation 6. No system is perfect, so use development in place for all managers. Development on one's present job can be enhanced by adding spice in the way of new challenges. On page 37 are 25 examples of development on one's present job (Lombardo & Eichinger, 1989). Many of these can be added to almost any management job. Hiring a small secretarial pool, being assigned an unfamiliar task or one where the last person to try failed, serving with the United Way, or settling an internal squabble are miniature versions of the larger challenges managers will eventually face.

Too often, organizations rely on rotational practices to develop new managers, but in retrospect current executives rarely see such assignments as having been pivotal. This seems to be because functional rotations provide vital business and technical knowledge but develop leadership skills only incidentally. In contrast, experiencing variety in leadership challenges and learning from those challenges is strongly related to effectiveness and promotion to the executive ranks. The unfortunate flip side also holds: Narrowness of experience derailed many otherwise talented managers.

Early exposure to leadership challenges also helps young managers like Michelle find out what they really like to do. Some will discover that they prefer technical challenges and some will realize the complexity involved in

25 DEVELOPMENT IN PLACE OPTIONS

A.   Mini-Project and Start-ups (emphasize persuasion and working with new people, leadership depends on if the person is in charge).

1. Plan an off-site meeting, conference, convention.
2. Handle a negotiation with a customer.
3. Work with a plant shut-down crew.
4. Go off-site to troubleshoot problems (e.g., deal with dissatisfied customer).
5. Launch new product/program.

B.   Mini-Scope Jumps and Fix-its (person has full responsibility, often emphasize pressure, leadership, dealing with the boss).

6. Team build—green staff.
7. Team build—balky staff.
8. Team build—subordinates are experts, person is not.
9. Deal with a business crisis.
10. Assign "undoable" project (last person who tried it failed).
11. Supervise cost-cutting.

C.   Mini-Strategy Assignments (emphasize intellectual pressure, influence, lacking credibility and strategy; they may or may not be closely watched by top management).

12. Write a proposal for a new system, product, etc.
13. Spend a week with customers/write report.
14. Do a competitive analysis.
15. Study innovation of customers/competitors.
16. Evaluate impact of training.

D.   Coursework/Coaching (tend to emphasize missing something, intellectual pressure which can lead to heightened self-awareness).

17. Design training course.
18. Attend self-awareness course.
19. Train as an assessor in assessment center.
20. Study history/draw business parallels.
21. Assign to work with higher manager who is particularly good or bad at something.

E.   Off-Job (tend to emphasize individual leadership, new people, and have a heavy influence/persuasion component).

22. Become active in a professional organization.
23. Serve with a community agency.
24. Act as a consultant on a problem/issue outside job.
25. Coach children's sports.

(From Lombardo & Eichinger, 1989)

leadership. Others will realize that they like one kind of leadership challenge but not others. Others will realize they're not interested in management, and still others will discover leadership talent no one suspected they had.

Becoming an Active Learner

Many managers have variety in their leadership experience and get excellent feedback, yet derail because try as they do, they cannot escape past habits.

Although they learn rapidly when confronted with technical challenges, they use the same management behaviors over and over. They know one way to build a team or use one or two motivational tactics. In brief, they are poor at making transitions. They apply old skills to new situations without asking "What's different here? What challenges do I face that require me to learn to do something differently? Must I learn to be strategic? To let go? To motivate a disgruntled staff? To hire people for the first time?"

While we might assume that any competent manager would automatically learn to behave differently, new learning is threatening. It's easier to rely on past habits and force-fit new challenges into old models. Such people often decide alone and control things tightly while giving lip service to how adaptable they are. In John Kotter's study, *The General Managers* (1982), all the GMs he worked with knew how to adapt, but only the effective ones put their knowledge into practice. Many younger managers are more like Michelle. They fear giving up comfortable habits, don't know how to be adaptable, and suffer from what they don't know how to do.

Whether managers *know* how to adapt (or don't), in the CCL studies only the executives who remained successful showed any pattern of new management learning from their experiences (McCall et al., 1988). As noted earlier, they usually learned to focus on developing subordinates once they got into a job that was quite complex. In contrast, derailed executives never mentioned this learning. They were more likely to turn to the boss for help, then try to figure out what was going on so they could control it themselves. In a sense they were prisoners of past successful habits and couldn't make the transition to new ways of behaving.

There are several ways to help more managers become what some managers are naturally—active learners of new management behavior.

Recommendation 7. Help managers become more aware of them-selves as learners willing to experiment with new behavior. The danger is always that a new task may be met with old behavior, using management techniques that worked well in the previous situation. In effect, managers need awareness of the developmental transition they are making and a plan for dealing with it.

To gain from the situation they need, of course, not only to try different things but to learn something from their efforts. Some examples of methods of helping managers learn from their experiences are:

- keeping a learning diary to understand when they learn well or don't, when their habitual ways of doing things work or don't;

- seeking tutoring from previous job incumbents;

- placing them with a role model who exemplifies how to do some-thing well;

- asking them what they have learned often, and what habits they have that are getting too comfortable for them;

- having regular dinner meetings with those who face or have faced similar leadership challenges;

- attending coursework targeted toward self-awareness of strengths, weaknesses and limits, or which addresses a compelling problem they face on the job at present;

- having them construct a learning plan (how will they size up people? team-build? create a symbol for change or rallying cry? deal with the boss?);

- receiving feedback on personality tests (like the *Myers-Briggs Type Indicator*) which help managers understand their preferred methods for learning and coping with the world.

Recommendation 8. Help managers to learn effectively. Following are some typical learning differences between those who derail prematurely because they fail to learn as much as they can from their management experi-

BLOCKS TO LEARNING	**AIDS TO LEARNING**
1. Focus on results and technical matters. Little attention paid to leadership role.	1. Focus on results and leadership challenges; often had a flexible plan for how they will lead.
2. Overcontrolling. May wipe out ambiguity or conflict with quick decisions or go to the other extreme and study problems into the ground. Uncomfortable with the fragmented pace of management work or "first time problems." May justify behavior by saying they're very busy.	2. Develop a tolerance for ambiguity and uncontrollable situations: remain open to different views of the problem, not jump to conclusions, rely on small experiments and feedback from them, take the time to work through conflicts.
3. Excessive reliance on bosses, high status figures or self for counsel. Not particularly open to feedback from others or fail to act on feedback.	3. Seek feedback from success or failure on tasks. May not seek but are open to feedback from many sources—boss, self, subordinates, peers, customers, etc.
4. Habit-bound—have a good sense of what worked in the past and try to repeat it. Like to work with same people, similar functions and technical areas. Show little interest in team-building in new situations or getting a mix of talents in the group.	4. Focus on the transition from one challenge to another. What habits have gotten too comfortable? What is different about this challenge that requires acting differently? What can be learned from this?
5. Overgeneralize, ". . . the way to develop people is . . ."; form precepts and fit new events within them.	5. Specify what one is learning—for example, nine different team-building situations were mentioned by successful executives in CCL research. While successful executives had a few general learnings about team-building, they were more likely than the derailed to mention lessons specific to each team-building situation.
6. Low self-awareness—not attuned to the interplay of strengths, weaknesses, and limits within self. May be reluctant to express or not know what strong likes and dislikes are.	6. Develop awareness of what strengths and weaknesses they have and how they are linked together. This can lead to the self-awareness necessary to make transitions to a different way of behaving.
7. Unaware of impact—may get abdicative, passive, dictatorial or abrasive under pressure, yet not know it or justify it by calling it something else.	7. Become aware of interpersonal impact. Are they trusted? Seen as volatile or calm? Through feedback and coursework, come to understand how small day-to-day actions have a large impact on others.

8. Take problems personally—may be seen as emotionally volatile under pressure.

8. Learn to talk about emotions, likes and dislikes, without overreacting. Stability under pressure and composure differentiated successful from derailed executives in the CCL studies.

9. Promotion-oriented—may openly plan for next job, politic, or not be particularly demanding of subordinates, which may leave them undeveloped.

9. Focus on solving problems in the job they're in rather than ticket-punching for the future. Successful executives were more likely to focus on present challenges, be quite demanding of subordinates and, partly due to that, often developed the talent beneath them.

10. Doesn't handle mistakes well—may sandbag, try to fix it without telling others, or lament it to the point where the mistake is dwelt on past all value. Often doesn't handle the mistakes and failures of others well either.

10. Learn to admit mistakes, warn those affected, learn from them, and move on to something else. As mentioned, it's relatively easy to blame others, the situation, not think much about our blunders, or to naively believe it will never happen again.

ences and those who are excellent learners. Such people much more often get to executive ranks and stay there, but our purpose here is to encourage not only progression but learning. Several studies have shown that it is not level or income that relates to life satisfaction but, among other reasons, being an active learner who seeks new challenges (Bray & Howard, 1988).

Learning from experience is a tough, never-ending task. Heightened awareness, trying different learning tactics, and removing blocks to effective learning are all necessary for growth. The learning process for Michelle did not have to wait for Marv.

Numerous bosses and learning tactics could have been offered to her earlier.

Conclusion

Although many potential derailers (and the already derailed) can be saved, some—even if they come to own the problem—decide fixing it is not important enough to them to make the effort.

Some decide to stick with what works for them and make the best of it. They do not want to make the transition from personal producer to manager or strategist. Others love to start operations from scratch *or* fix broken businesses *or* expand growing businesses, but are not interested in all of these challenges.

There are also some who truly wish to be executives but will derail despite the best efforts to help them. In our experience, their excessive reliance on self as a source of standards becomes an albatross. Such men and women have often done it all alone, are independent to a fault and don't trust others to provide them with helpful feedback. They appear immune to feedback and strongly defend their own view of themselves. These are the people afflicted with what John Kotter called the "I can do anything syndrome" (Kotter, 1982). Such managers tend to ignore other people's views, behave as if they have never failed, and are extremely unlikely to have had a mentor who demonstrated caring and understanding toward others.

Derailment is also the ebb and flow of life as personal priorities change or those who look good early opt out or seem to lack some essential ingredient in later career.

It's important to have frequent reassessments, however. Just as situations change, so do people. As the Michelles and others go through life and management transitions, their perspectives may change substantially. As the work of Eliot Jaques (1989) and Barbara Kovach (1986) shows, some capabilities increase with age. Older managers are often able to deal with greater complexity, and both can push their point of view and integrate the views of others better. As the works of Erikson and Levinson have shown (Erikson, 1963; Levinson, 1978), older managers are much more interested in nurturing others and "passing it on." So development takes time and some things cannot be rushed without the danger of derailing someone who is as yet unready. Recall that Michelle was only asked to work on her skills to have a better impact. She wasn't asked to have developing others as a major personal goal, a perspective unlikely to occur for some years.

Most young managers like Michelle are better off enhancing their skills, and letting perspective build from experience and maturation. Barbara Kovach's research indicates that the broad perspectives necessary to become effective at higher levels are best developed from a strong skill base that takes 15-20 years to mature. She concludes, "Americans have traditionally wanted to speed up all the developmental processes. They try to create first-rate readers at the age of three and first-rate executives at the age of thirty. The developmentalists tell us, however, that these processes can't be speeded up without undue cost in other areas" (Kovach, 1986).

Through timely feedback on an effectiveness and derailment profile, more variety in the leadership experience of managers, careful attention to how and what managers learn, and occasional intervention when managers get in trouble, fewer managers can derail.

If fewer managers derailed, organizations could save money. Estimates of unwanted turnover due to derailment costs run from six figures at middle management to seven figures at the senior executive level. Exit costs, wasted training and education, hiring costs, restart costs, and the cascade effect of one empty slot at the top leading to multiple position shuffles could diminish.

If fewer managers derailed, there could be less turnover and more opportunity to build team spirit and commitment that results from continuity and long-term service. Experience and perspective could build.

If fewer managers derailed, people could lead richer, more exciting, more satisfying lives with less displacement and pain.

If fewer managers derailed, our country could have a cadre of more truly qualified leaders.

References

The Center for Creative Leadership's studies of executive development began in 1982 and are continuing. Many publications have resulted from these investigations and have been referred to throughout this report.

The technical aspects of the interviews and surveys of key events and lessons are detailed in *Key Events in Executives' Lives* (1987) by Esther Lindsey, Virginia Homes, and Morgan McCall. A non-technical depiction of the studies, which contains several implications sections, was published in 1988 (*The Lessons of Experience* by Morgan McCall, Michael Lombardo, and Ann Morrison, Lexington Books).

Other studies: A companion interview study of executive women was published in 1987 by Addison-Wesley (*Breaking the Glass Ceiling* by Morrison, Randall White, and Ellen Van Velsor). Three studies of derailment—*Off The Track: Why and How Successful Executives Get Derailed* (McCall and Lombardo), "Explanations of Success and Derailment in Upper-Level Management Positions" (Lombardo, Marian Ruderman, and Cynthia McCauley, *Journal of Business and Psychology*, 1988), and *The Dynamics of Management Derailment* (Lombardo and McCauley, 1988a)—have been published. A summary and interpretation of the values-oriented events, *Values in Action: The Meaning of Executive Vignettes* (Lombardo, 1986); a description and interpretation of other research into development experiences for managers, *Developmental Experiences in Managerial Work* (McCauley, 1986); an inventory measuring executive lessons, derailment factors, and challenging jobs, *Benchmarks®* (Lombardo and McCauley, 1988b); and a technical article describing the development of Benchmarks®, "Diagnosing Management Development Needs: An Instrument Based on How Managers Develop" (*Journal of Management*, forthcoming) by McCauley, Lombardo, and Claire Usher have been published. Developing managers on their present jobs is discussed in *Eighty-eight Assignments for Development in Place* (Lombardo and Robert Eichinger, 1989). All are available from Center for Creative Leadership Publications, P.O. Box 26300, Greensboro, NC 27438-6300, (910) 545-2805.

We also drew heavily on the AT&T studies of career progress. Beginning in 1956, AT&T followed a group of men (women managers were added in the 1970s), studying the contribution to career progress of personality variables, relationships between income, level and life satisfaction, skills and abilities, and changing motivational patterns in the management population. Excellent summaries of these studies are contained in Ann Howard and Doug Bray's book, *Management Lives in Transition* (Guilford Press, 1988); Bray, Richard Campbell, and Don Grant, *Formative Years in Business* (Wiley, 1974); Manuel London, "Development for New Managers" (*Journal of Management Development*, Vol. 2, No. 4, 1983); and Kerry Bunker, "Tackling Stress and Lifestyle Problems of Women in Management," A. M. Morrison (Chair), Developing Top Business Women: What Helps and What Hurts (APA Symposium, August 1987).

Other studies we relied on include Bernard Bass's *Leadership and Performance Beyond Expectations* (Free Press, 1985); Jon Bentz's reports on the Sears studies of executive effectiveness, particularly "Research Findings from Personality Assessment of Executives" (presentation to Human Resource Planning Society Conference, 1986); and David DeVries, Morrison, Sandra Shullman, and Michael Gerlach, *Performance Appraisal on the Line,* for reviews of managerial appraisal and feedback (Wiley, 1981).

We relied on many studies concerning development (or the lack of it) across time: Robert Kaplan, Wilfred Drath, and Joan Kofodimos, *High Hurdles* (CCL, 1985); Barbara Kovach, "The Derailment of Fast-Track Managers" (*Organizational Dynamics*, Autumn 1986) and *Survival on the Fast Track* (Dodd, 1988); E. H. Erikson, *Childhood and Society* (Norton, 1963); Warren Bennis and Burt Nanus, *Leaders* (Harper & Row, 1985); Mel Sorcher, *Predicting Executive Success* (Wiley, 1985); D. J. Levinson, *The Seasons of a Man's Life* (Ballantine Books, 1978); Eliot Jaques, *Requisite Organization* (Cason Hall & Co., 1989); John Kotter, *Power and Influence* (1985), *The General Managers* (1982), and *The Leadership Factor* (1988), all published by Free Press; Jack Gabarro, *The Dynamics of Taking Charge* (Harvard Business School Press, 1987); James Kouzes and Barry Posner, *The Leadership Challenge* (Jossey-Bass, 1987); and Thomas Peters, *Thriving on Chaos* (Random House, 1987).

We also referred to studies of using practical intelligence in new learning situations: Richard Wagner and Robert Sternberg, "Practical Intelligence in Real World Pursuits: The Role of Tacit Knowledge" (*Journal of Personality and Social Psychology*, Vol. 49, No. 2, 1985) and "Tacit Knowledge and Managerial Success" (*Journal of Business and Psychology*, Vol. 1, No. 4, 1987).

Appendix
Leadership Effectiveness Factors

	Description of Scale	Sample Items
HANDLING THE DEMANDS OF THE MANAGEMENT JOB		
1. RESOURCEFULNESS	Can think strategically, engage in flexible problem-solving behavior, and work effectively with higher management.	• makes good decisions under pressure with incomplete information • links his/her responsibilities with the mission of the whole organization
2. DOING WHATEVER IT TAKES	Has perseverance and focus in the face of obstacles.	• faces difficult situations with guts and tenacity • controls his/her own career; does not sit and wait for the company to plan a course to follow
3. BEING A QUICK STUDY	Quickly masters new technical and business knowledge.	• learns a new skill quickly • quickly masters new vocabulary and operating rules needed to understand how the business works
4. DECISIVENESS	Prefers quick and approximate actions to slow and precise ones in many management situations.	• displays a real bias for action, calculated risks, and quick decisions • does not hesitate when making decisions
DEALING WITH SUBORDINATES		
5. LEADING SUBORDINATES	Delegates to subordinates effectively, broadens their opportunities, and acts with fairness toward them.	• is willing to delegate important tasks, not just things he/she doesn't want to do • relies on persuasion or expertise first; uses the power of the position as a last resort
6. SETTING A DEVELOPMENTAL CLIMATE	Provides a challenging climate to encourage subordinates' development.	• is willing to pitch in and lead subordinates by example • develops subordinates by providing challenge and opportunity

7. CONFRONTING PROBLEM SUBORDINATES	Acts decisively and with fairness when dealing with problem subordinates.	• is able to fire loyal but incompetent people without procrastinating • can deal effectively with resistant subordinates
8. WORK TEAM ORIENTATION	Accomplishes tasks through managing others.	• acts as if his/her managerial success is built by a team of strong subordinates
9. HIRING TALENTED STAFF	Hires talented people for his/her team.	• hires people who are not afraid of responsibility or risks

RESPECT FOR SELF AND OTHERS

10. BUILDING AND MENDING RELATIONSHIPS	Knows how to build and maintain working relationships with co-workers and external parties.	• when working with a group over whom he/she has no control, gets things done by finding common ground • relates to all kinds of individuals tactfully, from shop floor to top executives
11. COMPASSION AND SENSITIVITY	Shows genuine interest in others and sensitivity to subordinates' needs.	• is willing to help an employee with personal problems • is sensitive to signs of overwork in others
12. STRAIGHTFOR-WARDNESS AND COMPOSURE	Is honorable and steadfast.	• relies on style more than substance in dealings with top management • becomes hostile or moody when things are not going his/her way
13. BALANCE BE-TWEEN PERSONAL LIFE AND WORK	Balances work priorities with personal life so that neither is neglected.	• acts as if there is more to life than just having a career • lets job demands cause family problems
14. SELF-AWARENESS	Has an accurate picture of strengths and weaknesses and is willing to improve.	• sorts out his/her strengths and weaknesses fairly accurately
15. PUTTING PEOPLE AT EASE	Displays warmth and a good sense of humor.	• has a warm personality that puts people at ease
16. ACTING WITH FLEXIBILITY	Can behave in ways that are often seen as opposites.	• is tough and at the same time compassionate • can lead and let others lead

CENTER FOR CREATIVE LEADERSHIP PUBLICATIONS LIST

NEW RELEASES

IDEAS INTO ACTION GUIDEBOOKS

Ongoing Feedback: How to Get It, How to Use It Kirkland & Manoogian (1998, Stock #400) $8.95*

Reaching Your Development Goals McCauley & Martineau (1998, Stock #401) $8.95*

Becoming a More Versatile Learner Dalton (1998, Stock #402) $8.95

Giving Feedback to Subordinates Buron & McDonald-Mann (1999, Stock #403) $8.95*

Three Keys to Development: Using Assessment, Challenge, and Support to Drive Your Leadership
Browning & Van Velsor (1999, Stock #404) $8.95*

Feedback That Works: How to Build and Deliver Your Message Weitzel (2000, Stock #405) $8.95*

Communicating Across Cultures Prince & Hoppe (2000, Stock #406) $8.95

Learning From Life: Turning Life's Lessons into Leadership Experience Ruderman & Ohlott
(2000, Stock #407) $8.95

Keeping Your Career on Track: Twenty Success Strategies Chappelow & Leslie (2001, Stock #408) $8.95

Preparing for Development: Making the Most of Formal Leadership Programs Martineau & Johnson
(2001, Stock #409) $8.95*

Choosing an Executive Coach Kirkland & Hart (2001, Stock #410) $8.95

Setting Your Development Goals: Start with Your Values Sternbergh & Weitzel (2001, Stock #411) $8.95*

Do You Really Need a Team? Kossler & Kanaga (2001, Stock #412) $8.95

Building Resiliency: How to Thrive in Times of Change Pulley & Wakefield (2001, Stock #413) $8.95

The Deep Blue Sea: Rethinking the Source of Leadership Drath (2001, Stock #2068) $27.95

Discovering the Leader in You Lee & King (2001, Stock #2067) $32.95

Emerging Leaders: An Annotated Bibliography Deal, Peterson, & Gaylor-Loflin (2001, Stock #352) $20.00

Executive Coaching: An Annotated Bibliography Douglas & Morley (2000, Stock #347) $20.00*

Executive Selection: Strategies for Success Sessa & Taylor (2000, Stock #2057) $34.95*

The Human Side of Knowledge Management: An Annotated Bibliography Mayer (2000, Stock #349) $20.00

Leadership Resources: A Guide to Training and Development Tools (8th ed.) Schwartz & Gimbel
(2000, Stock #348) $49.95*

BEST-SELLERS

Breaking Free: A Prescription for Personal and Organizational Change Noer (1997, Stock #271) $25.00

Breaking the Glass Ceiling: Can Women Reach the Top of America's Largest Corporations?
(Updated Edition) Morrison, White, & Van Velsor (1992, Stock #236A) $13.00

The Center for Creative Leadership Handbook of Leadership Development McCauley, Moxley,
& Van Velsor (Eds.) (1998, Stock #201) $75.00*

Choosing 360: A Guide to Evaluating Multi-rater Feedback Instruments for Management
Development Van Velsor, Leslie, & Fleenor (1997, Stock #334) $15.00*

Choosing Executives: A Research Report on the Peak Selection Simulation Deal, Sessa, & Taylor
(1999, Stock #183) $20.00*

Coaching for Action: A Report on Long-term Advising in a Program Context Guthrie (1999, Stock #181) $20.00*

The Complete Inklings: Columns on Leadership and Creativity Campbell (1999, Stock #343) $20.00

Eighty-eight Assignments for Development in Place Lombardo & Eichinger (1989, Stock #136) $15.00*

Enhancing 360-degree Feedback for Senior Executives: How to Maximize the Benefits and Minimize
the Risks Kaplan & Palus (1994, Stock #160) $7.50*

Executive Selection: A Research Report on What Works and What Doesn't Sessa, Kaiser,Taylor, &
Campbell (1998, Stock #179) $30.00*

Feedback to Managers (3rd Edition) Leslie & Fleenor (1998, Stock #178) $20.00*

Four Essential Ways that Coaching Can Help Executives Witherspoon & White (1997, Stock #175) $10.00

High Flyers: Developing the Next Generation of Leaders McCall (1997, Stock #293) $27.95

How to Design an Effective System for Developing Managers and Executives Dalton & Hollenbeck
(1996, Stock #158) $15.00*

If I'm In Charge Here, Why Is Everybody Laughing? Campbell (1984, Stock #205) $9.95*

If You Don't Know Where You're Going You'll Probably End Up Somewhere Else Campbell (1974, Stock #203) $9.95*

Internalizing Strengths: An Overlooked Way of Overcoming Weaknesses in Managers Kaplan (1999, Stock #182) $15.00

International Success: Selecting, Developing, and Supporting Expatriate Managers Wilson & Dalton (1998, Stock #180) $15.00*

Leadership and Spirit Moxley (1999, Stock #2035) $35.00

The Lessons of Experience: How Successful Executives Develop on the Job McCall, Lombardo, & Morrison (1988, Stock #211) $28.00

Making Common Sense: Leadership as Meaning-making in a Community of Practice Drath & Palus (1994, Stock #156) $15.00

Maximizing the Value of 360-degree Feedback Tornow, London, & CCL Associates (1998, Stock #295) $45.00*

Perspectives on Dialogue: Making Talk Developmental for Individuals and Organizations Dixon (1996, Stock #168) $20.00

Positive Turbulence: Developing Climates for Creativity, Innovation, and Renewal Gryskiewicz (1999, Stock #2031) $35.00

Preventing Derailment: What To Do Before It's Too Late Lombardo & Eichinger (1989, Stock #138) ... $25.00

Selected Research on Work Team Diversity Ruderman, Hughes-James, & Jackson (Eds.) (1996, Stock #326) $24.95

Should 360-degree Feedback Be Used Only for Developmental Purposes? Bracken, Dalton, Jako, McCauley, Pollman, with Preface by Hollenbeck (1997, Stock #335) $15.00*

Take the Road to Creativity and Get Off Your Dead End Campbell (1977, Stock #204) $9.95*

Twenty-two Ways to Develop Leadership in Staff Managers Eichinger & Lombardo (1990, Stock #144) $15.00

BIBLIOGRAPHIES

Formal Mentoring Programs in Organizations: An Annotated Bibliography Douglas (1997, Stock #332) $20.00

Geographically Dispersed Teams: An Annotated Bibliography Sessa, Hansen, Prestridge, & Kossler (1999, Stock #346) $20.00*

High-Performance Work Organizations: Definitions, Practices, and an Annotated Bibliography Kirkman, Lowe, & Young (1999, Stock #342) $20.00

Management Development through Job Experiences: An Annotated Bibliography McCauley & Brutus (1998, Stock #337) $10.00

Selecting International Executives: A Suggested Framework and Annotated Bibliography London & Sessa (1999, Stock #345) $20.00

Selection at the Top: An Annotated Bibliography Sessa & Campbell (1997, Stock #333) $20.00*

Succession Planning: An Annotated Bibliography Eastman (1995, Stock #324) $20.00*

Using 360-degree Feedback in Organizations: An Annotated Bibliography Fleenor & Prince (1997, Stock #338) $15.00*

Workforce Reductions: An Annotated Bibliography Hickok (1999, Stock #344) $20.00*

SPECIAL PACKAGES

Executive Selection Package (Stock #710C; includes 157, 164, 179, 180, 183, 333, 345, 2057) $100.00

Feedback Guidebook Package (Stock #724; includes 400, 403, 405) $17.95

Human Resource Professionals Information Package (Stock #717C; includes 136, 158, 179, 180, 182, 201, 324, 334, 348—includes complimentary copy of guidebook 409) $150.00

Individual Leadership Development Package (Stock #726; includes 401, 404, 409, 411) $26.95

Personal Growth, Taking Charge, and Enhancing Creativity (Stock #231; includes 203, 204, 205) $25.00

Select Sourcebook Package (Stock #727; includes 178, 324, 344, 346, 347, 348) $100.00

The 360 Collection (Stock #720C; includes 160, 178, 295, 334, 335, 338—includes complimentary copies of guidebooks contained in Feedback Guidebook Package above) $100.00

Discounts are available. Please write for a catalog. Address your request to: Publication, Center for Creative Leadership, P.O. Box 26300, Greensboro, NC 27438-6300, 336-545-2810, or fax to 336-282-3284. Purchase your publications from our online bookstore at **www.ccl.org/publications**. All prices subject to change.

*Indicates publication is also part of a package.

11/01

ORDER FORM

Or e-mail your order via the Center's online bookstore at www.ccl.org

Name _____ Title _____

Organization _____

Mailing Address _____
(street address required for mailing)

City/State/Zip _____

Telephone _____ FAX _____
(telephone number required for UPS mailing)

Quantity	Stock No.	Title	Unit Cost	Amount

CCL's Federal ID Number
is 237-07-9591.

Subtotal

Shipping and Handling
(U.S. shipping rate $4 for 1st book, $0.95 for each additional book;
International shipping rate $20 for 1st book, $5 for each additional book)

NC residents add 6.5% sales tax; CA residents add
7.5% sales tax; CO residents add 6% sales tax

TOTAL

METHOD OF PAYMENT
(ALL orders for less than $100 must be PREPAID.)

❏ Check or money order enclosed (payable to Center for Creative Leadership).

❏ Purchase Order No. _____ (Must be accompanied by this form.)

❏ Charge my order, plus shipping, to my credit card:
        ❏ American Express   ❏ Discover   ❏ MasterCard   ❏ Visa

ACCOUNT NUMBER:_____ EXPIRATION DATE: MO.___ YR.___

NAME AS APPEARS ON CARD: _____

SIGNATURE OF CARD HOLDER: _____

❏ Please put me on your mailing list.

**Publication • Center for Creative Leadership • P.O. Box 26300
Greensboro, NC 27438-6300
336-545-2810 • FAX 336-282-3284**

fold here

CENTER FOR CREATIVE LEADERSHIP
PUBLICATION
P.O. Box 26300
Greensboro, NC 27438-6300